THE BIG GAME

THE WORLD SERIES

BASEBALL'S FALL CLASSIC

Lerner Publications Company
An imprint of Lerner Publishing Group, Inc.
241 First Avenue North
Minneapolis, MN 55401 USA

For reading levels and more information, look up this title at www.lernerbooks.com.

Main body text set in Conduit ITC Std.
Typeface provided by International Typeface Corp.

Designer: Viet Chu

Library of Congress Cataloging-in-Publication Data

Names: Scheff, Matt, author. | Lerner Publications Company.
Title: The World Series : baseball's Fall classic / Matt Scheff.
Other titles: Baseball's Fall classic
Description: Minneapolis, Minnesota : Lerner Publications, 2020. | Series: The big game (Lerner Sports) | Includes bibliographical references and index. | Audience: Ages: 7–11 years | Audience: Grades: 2–3 | Summary: "Read about the biggest baseball games, the most thrilling moments, and the greatest players in World Series history"— Provided by publisher.
Identifiers: LCCN 2019041626 (print) | LCCN 2019041627 (ebook) | ISBN 9781541597549 (Library Binding) | ISBN 9781728401287 (eBook)
Subjects: LCSH: World Series (Baseball)—History—Juvenile literature.
Classification: LCC GV878.4 .S32 2020 (print) | LCC GV878.4 (ebook) | DDC 796.357/646—dc23

LC record available at https://lccn.loc.gov/2019041626
LC ebook record available at https://lccn.loc.gov/2019041627

Manufactured in the United States of America
1-47858-48298-1/30/2020

Contents

Fans filled the seats at Progressive Field in Cleveland for Game 7 of the 2016 World Series.

THE WAIT IS OVER

The Cleveland, Ohio, crowd was buzzing. It was the 10th inning of Game 7 of the 2016 World Series. The Cleveland Indians and the Chicago Cubs were tied 6–6. Chicago's Ben Zobrist stepped to the plate with a runner on second base.

Zobrist slapped the ball to left field, driving in the go-ahead run. The Cubs added a second run for an 8–6 lead. Just three outs separated them from a championship.

Cleveland scored a run in the bottom of the 10th. But with a runner on first base, the Cubs got the final out. They stormed the field to celebrate. It was Chicago's first World Series title in more than 100 years. The drama reminded fans everywhere why the World Series is called the Fall Classic.

Facts at a Glance

- The New York Yankees won 19 World Series titles from 1927 to 1962.

- In 2011, the St. Louis Cardinals were one strike away from losing the World Series. But they came back to beat the Texas Rangers and win the title.

- San Francisco Giants pitcher Madison Bumgarner has dominated the Fall Classic. In 36 World Series innings pitched, he has allowed just one earned run.

- In 2016, almost 32 million people watched the Chicago Cubs beat the Cleveland Indians in Game 7 of the World Series.

On October 1, 1903, the Pittsburgh Pirates beat the Boston Americans 7-3 at Boston's Huntington Avenue Grounds in the first World Series game.

CHAPTER 1

THE FALL CLASSIC

IN THE EARLY 1900S, TWO RIVAL PRO BASEBALL LEAGUES, the National League (NL) and the American League (AL), competed for attention. In 1903, the NL champion Pittsburgh Pirates met the AL champion Boston Americans in a series to determine the world's best baseball team. An October tradition was born.

THE EVOLVING GAME

Dynasties marked the early years of the World Series. The Philadelphia Athletics and Boston Red Sox took turns on top in the 1910s. In 1919, the Red Sox sold a young pitcher named Babe Ruth to the New York Yankees. The Yankees turned Ruth into a hitter, and he went on to rewrite the record books. He helped launch a Yankees dynasty that won 19 Fall Classics between 1927 and 1962.

Babe Ruth

Inside the Game

In 1919, gamblers paid eight members of the Chicago White Sox to lose the Word Series on purpose. After the Cincinnati Reds won the series, MLB caught and banned from the game the Chicago players who took money. Fans remember it as the Black Sox Scandal.

The 1940s and 1950s brought change to the game. Infielder Jackie Robinson broke Major League Baseball's (MLB) color barrier in 1947. MLB had banned players of color for more than 50 years. Robinson opened the door for black superstars such as Willie Mays and Bob Gibson.

Jackie Robinson played ten seasons for Brooklyn and helped the Dodgers beat the Yankees in the 1955 World Series.

In 2019, Stephen Strasburg led the Washington Nationals to their first World Series title.

In 1969, MLB introduced a new playoff format. Until then, the AL and NL regular-season champions had gone to the World Series. The new format split each league into two divisions and added a round to the playoffs. By 2012, five teams from each league made the playoffs each season.

Most fans loved the expanded playoffs. Nothing beats playoff baseball, and the road to the World Series is filled with fascinating twists and turns. Since almost a third of the league makes the postseason each year, fans everywhere can dream that their favorite team will be the next World Series champion.

In eight career World Series games, Bill Mazeroski had a .308 batting average and hit two home runs.

CHAPTER 2

GREATEST MOMENTS

MORE THAN A CENTURY OF WORLD SERIES GAMES has provided countless thrills. But a few stand above the rest. Read on to learn more about some of the greatest moments in the history of the Fall Classic.

Maz Walks Off

Some reporters called Game 7 of the 1960 World Series the greatest game ever played. It was a back-and-forth nail-biter. The underdog Pittsburgh Pirates jumped out to a 4–0 lead. The Yankees stormed back with a flurry of runs, only to see Pittsburgh reclaim the lead with a five-run eighth inning.

By the time Pittsburgh batted in the bottom of the ninth inning, the score was tied 9–9. Second baseman Bill (Maz) Mazeroski stepped to the plate. Maz wasn't a big slugger. But he took a mighty swing at the pitch. *Crack!* Maz crushed the ball over the left-field fence for a home run. Fans and teammates mobbed him at home plate to celebrate the only Game 7 walk-off home run in World Series history.

Mazeroski raises his arm in celebration as he approaches home plate.

On One Leg

The Los Angeles Dodgers were in trouble in Game 1 of the 1988 World Series. They trailed the Oakland A's 4–3 in the bottom of the ninth inning. Dennis Eckersley, one of the greatest closers in history, pitched for the A's.

Eckersley got two outs before walking a batter. Los Angeles's best hitter, NL Most Valuable Player (MVP) Kirk Gibson, was on the bench with a leg injury. Manager Tommy Lasorda knew Gibson couldn't run. But he could still swing a bat. So Lasorda sent him to the plate.

Dennis Eckersley began his career as a starting pitcher before becoming a closer in 1987.

Gibson limped to home plate. With three balls and two strikes, he took a mighty hack. It was an awkward, off balance, one-legged swing. But Gibson connected. The ball sailed over the right-field fence for a home run as Dodgers fans celebrated one of the most shocking World Series moments ever.

Gibson smashes the game-winning home run.

Inside the Game

One of the most memorable—and crushing—World Series moments came in 1986. The Boston Red Sox almost won it all in Game 6. But first baseman Bill Buckner let a ground ball roll between his legs. The New York Mets scored on the play, winning the game and the series two days later.

PUCKETT'S PROMISE

The Minnesota Twins trailed the Atlanta Braves three games to two in the 1991 World Series. That was when star outfielder Kirby Puckett told his teammates to climb on his back. He was going to carry them to victory in Game 6.

Puckett delivered on his promise. First, he made a leaping catch to rob Atlanta's Ron Gant of an extra-base hit. Then, in the 11th inning, he slugged a walk-off home run. Puckett's heroics set up another great World Series game. In Game 7, Twins starter Jack Morris threw 10 scoreless innings before the Twins won on a walk-off single.

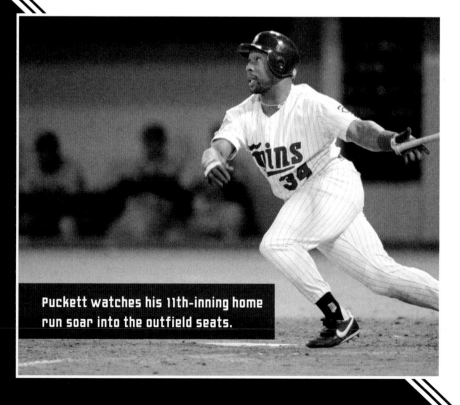

Puckett watches his 11th-inning home run soar into the outfield seats.

Puckett celebrates with teammates after winning Game 6.

COMEBACK KIDS

The 2011 St. Louis Cardinals made a habit of staging big comebacks. Their biggest came in Game 6 of the World Series. The Texas Rangers held a one-game lead. In the bottom of the ninth, trailing by two runs, the Cardinals' David Freese batted. Freese lined a pitch over a leaping defender. Two runners scored, sending the game to extra innings.

Freese watches his game-winning home run fly over the outfield fence.

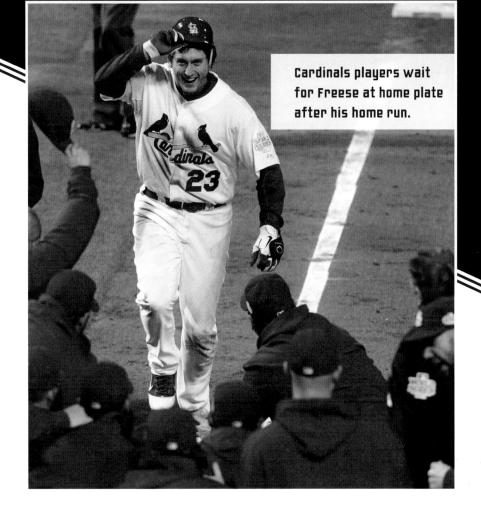

Cardinals players wait for Freese at home plate after his home run.

The Rangers reclaimed the lead in the 10th inning. The Cardinals were a strike away from losing the World Series. But Lance Berkman drilled a single to send the game to the 11th inning. After Texas failed to score, Freese batted again. This time, he blasted it over the center-field fence. The Cardinals won in one of the most amazing comebacks in MLB history. They went on to win Game 7 and the World Series.

Mariano Rivera recorded 652 career saves, the most in MLB history.

CHAPTER 3

CLUTCH
PERFORMERS

 OME PLAYERS ARE AT THEIR BEST WHEN THE LIGHTS shine brightest. Average players become stars. Stars become legends. Clutch performers in the World Series win championships and leave their mark on the game forever.

LOU GEHRIG

Lou Gehrig, nicknamed the Iron Horse, was the heart of the Yankees dynasty of the 1920s and 1930s. Gehrig played in seven World Series, winning six of them. In the 1928 series, he had a jaw-dropping .545 batting average. In 1932, he batted .529. That's clutch!

YOGI BERRA

No MLB player has more championships than Yogi Berra has. The Yankees legend won the Fall Classic 10 times. His greatest World Series came in 1953 when he batted .429.

BOB GIBSON

Flamethrower Bob Gibson led the Cardinals to World Series titles in 1964 and 1967. The Cardinals lost the 1968 World Series, but Gibson turned in a record-breaking performance in Game 1, striking out 17 hitters. In nine World Series games, Gibson had a 7–2 record and struck out 92 batters.

REGGIE JACKSON

Slugger Reggie Jackson was so clutch in the World Series he earned the nickname Mr. October. Jackson helped the Oakland A's win three titles in the early 1970s. Then he signed with the Yankees and played a series for the ages. Jackson belted five home runs in the 1977 World Series, including three in Game 6.

MARIANO RIVERA

Mariano Rivera was the greatest closer in World Series history. When he came into the game, it was all but over. Rivera won five World Series with the Yankees. Along the way, he racked up 11 saves—a World Series record.

MADISON BUMGARNER

Madison Bumgarner dominated the 2014 World Series. The San Francisco Giants pitcher helped beat the Kansas City Royals in Game 1. Next, he shut them out in Game 5. Then he threw five scoreless innings to close Game 7 and give San Francisco the championship! In 36 career World Series innings, Bumgarner has allowed only one run.

DAVID ORTIZ

David "Big Papi" Ortiz came to the World Series in style. He slugged a home run in his first World Series at bat and never looked back. Big Papi won three championships with the Red Sox, earning World Series MVP honors in 2013. In 14 World Series games, Ortiz batted a scorching .455 with three home runs.

GEORGE SPRINGER

Few players have played in a World Series as Houston Astros outfielder George Springer did in 2017. Springer crushed the Los Angeles Dodgers' pitching with a record-tying five home runs, including one in Houston's Game 7 victory. Springer took home the series MVP award.

Astros fans stand and cheer during the 2019 World Series.

Astros fans stand and cheer during the 2019 World Series.

CHAPTER 4

WORLD SERIES CULTURE

VERY WORLD SERIES GAME IS A SELLOUT. THE STANDS are packed. Fans come dressed in team colors, many wearing the jerseys of their favorite players. The smell of hot dogs and popcorn fills the air. People sell food, drinks, and souvenirs as fans find their seats.

In many cities, the October air is cool and crisp. The crowd stands for the national anthem and roars as the players run onto the field. That roar grows as the game begins—especially when the home team scores a run.

Singer and TV star Nicole Scherzinger sings the national anthem at Game 1 of the 2019 World Series.

Inside the Game

The World Series draws millions of viewers on television and social media. In 2016, almost 32 million people tuned in to watch the Cubs win Game 7. A year later, about 28 million people watched the Astros beat the Dodgers.

After the final out of the World Series, the winning team storms the field. The party carries on into the clubhouse. The winners receive the Commissioner's Trophy, and one player wins the series MVP award.

Red Sox outfielder Jackie Bradley Jr. celebrates with the Commissioner's Trophy in 2018.

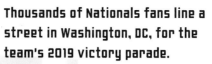

Thousands of Nationals fans line a street in Washington, DC, for the team's 2019 victory parade.

Many fans take to the streets to celebrate together. A few days after the game, they line up for a victory parade and one last chance to cheer on the players and coaches.

THE CHAMPIONS

Year	Champion	Year	Champion
2019	Washington Nationals	1990	Cincinnati Reds
2018	Boston Red Sox	1989	Oakland Athletics
2017	Houston Astros	1988	Los Angeles Dodgers
2016	Chicago Cubs	1987	Minnesota Twins
2015	Kansas City Royals	1986	New York Mets
2014	San Francisco Giants	1985	Kansas City Royals
2013	Boston Red Sox	1984	Detroit Tigers
2012	San Francisco Giants	1983	Baltimore Orioles
2011	St. Louis Cardinals	1982	St. Louis Cardinals
2010	San Francisco Giants	1981	Los Angeles Dodgers
2009	New York Yankees	1980	Philadelphia Phillies
2008	Philadelphia Phillies	1979	Pittsburgh Pirates
2007	Boston Red Sox	1978	New York Yankees
2006	St. Louis Cardinals	1977	New York Yankees
2005	Chicago White Sox	1976	Cincinnati Reds
2004	Boston Red Sox	1975	Cincinnati Reds
2003	Florida Marlins	1974	Oakland Athletics
2002	Anaheim Angels	1973	Oakland Athletics
2001	Arizona Diamondbacks	1972	Oakland Athletics
2000	New York Yankees	1971	Pittsburgh Pirates
1999	New York Yankees	1970	Baltimore Orioles
1998	New York Yankees	1969	New York Mets
1997	Florida Marlins	1968	Detroit Tigers
1996	New York Yankees	1967	St. Louis Cardinals
1995	Atlanta Braves	1966	Baltimore Orioles
1994	no World Series due to labor dispute	1965	Los Angeles Dodgers
		1964	St. Louis Cardinals
1993	Toronto Blue Jays	1963	Los Angeles Dodgers
1992	Toronto Blue Jays	1962	New York Yankees
1991	Minnesota Twins	1961	New York Yankees

Year	Champion	Year	Champion
1960	Pittsburgh Pirates	1931	St. Louis Cardinals
1959	Los Angeles Dodgers	1930	Philadelphia Athletics
1958	New York Yankees	1929	Philadelphia Athletics
1957	Milwaukee Braves	1928	New York Yankees
1956	New York Yankees	1927	New York Yankees
1955	Brooklyn Dodgers	1926	St. Louis Cardinals
1954	New York Giants	1925	Pittsburgh Pirates
1953	New York Yankees	1924	Washington Senators
1952	New York Yankees	1923	New York Yankees
1951	New York Yankees	1922	New York Giants
1950	New York Yankees	1921	New York Giants
1949	New York Yankees	1920	Cleveland Indians
1948	Cleveland Indians	1919	Cincinnati Reds
1947	New York Yankees	1918	Boston Red Sox
1946	St. Louis Cardinals	1917	Chicago White Sox
1945	Detroit Tigers	1916	Boston Red Sox
1944	St. Louis Cardinals	1915	Boston Red Sox
1943	New York Yankees	1914	Boston Braves
1942	St. Louis Cardinals	1913	Philadelphia Athletics
1941	New York Yankees	1912	Boston Red Sox
1940	Cincinnati Reds	1911	Philadelphia Athletics
1939	New York Yankees	1910	Philadelphia Athletics
1938	New York Yankees	1909	Pittsburgh Pirates
1937	New York Yankees	1908	Chicago Cubs
1936	New York Yankees	1907	Chicago Cubs
1935	Detroit Tigers	1906	Chicago White Sox
1934	St. Louis Cardinals	1905	New York Giants
1933	New York Giants	1904	no World Series
1932	New York Yankees	1903	Boston Americans

Glossary

batting average: a ratio of base hits to official times at bat

closer: a relief pitcher who specializes in finishing games

clutch: having the ability to perform in high-pressure situations

dynasty: a team that enjoys long-term success with multiple championships

playoffs: a series of contests played after the regular season to determine a champion

souvenir: something kept as a reminder of a place one has visited

underdog: a team that is not expected to win

upset: a game or series in which an underdog wins

walk-off: a play in which a home team scores a run in the bottom of the ninth inning or extra innings to win a game

Further Information

Baseball Hall of Fame
https://baseballhall.org

Cho, Alan. *World Series*. New York: AV2 by Weigl, 2020.

Fishman, Jon M. *Baseball's G.O.A.T.: Babe Ruth, Mike Trout, and More.*
Minneapolis: Lerner Publications, 2020.

Major League Baseball
http://mlb.com

Morey, Allan. *The World Series*. Minneapolis: Bellwether Media, 2019.

Sports Illustrated Kids—Baseball
https://www.sikids.com/baseball

Index

Photo Acknowledgments

Image credits: Tim Warner/Getty Images, p. 1; Tim Bradbury/Getty Images, p. 4; Todd Strand/Independent Picture Service, p. 5; Transcendental Graphics/Getty Images, pp. 6, 7; Photo File/Hulton Archive/Getty Images, pp. 8, 19; Bob Levey/Getty Images, p. 9; Bettmann/Getty Images, p. 10; Bruce Bennett/Getty Images, p. 11; AP Photo/Bob Galbraith, p. 12; Focus on Sport/Getty Images, pp. 13, 15, 20 (bottom), 21 (top); AP Photo/Jim Mone, p. 14; Rob Carr/Getty Images, p. 16; Ron T. Ennis/Fort Worth Star-Telegram/Tribune News Service/Getty Images, p. 17; J. Meric/Getty Images, pp. 18, 21 (bottom); Archive Photos/Getty Images, p. 20 (top); Dilip Vishwanat/Getty Images, p. 22 (top); Rich Gagnon/Getty Images, p. 22 (bottom); Jim McIsaac/Getty Images, p. 23; Cooper Neill/MLB Photos/Getty Images, p. 24; Alex Trautwig/MLB Photos/Getty Images, p. 25; Billie Weiss/Boston Red Sox/Getty Images, p. 26; Stefani Reynolds/Getty Images, p. 27. Design elements: tamjai9/Getty Images; zhengshun tang/Getty Images; Tuomas Lehtinen/Getty Images. Cover: Tim Warner/Getty Images.